The Gourd Dancer

Also by N. Scott Momaday

House Made of Dawn

The Way to Rainy Mountain

Angle of Geese and Other Poems

N. Scott Momaday

THE GOURD DANCER

Drawings by the Author

Harper & Row, Publishers
New York, Hagerstown, San Francisco, London

Some of the poems in this book have previously appeared in the following publications: *Oklahoma Today, The New Mexico Quarterly, North Country, Pembroke Magazine, Sequoia, The Southern Review, Angle of Geese and Other Poems* (David R. Godine, 1974), *Carriers of the Dream Wheel* (Harper & Row, 1975), and *The Way to Rainy Mountain* (The University of New Mexico Press, 1969).

FIRST EDITION

Designed by Gloria Adelson

Library of Congress Cataloging in Publication Data

Momaday, N. Scott, 1934–
  The gourd dancer.
  I. Title.
PS3563.047G6   811'.5'4   75–30338
ISBN 0–06–012982–4
ISBN 0–06–012983–2 pbk.

76 77 78 79 10 9 8 7 6 5 4 3 2 1

Contents

I

Angle of Geese

For Cael

The Bear

What ruse of vision,
escarping the wall of leaves,
rending incision
into countless surfaces,

would cull and color
his somnolence, whose old age
has outworn valor,
all but the fact of courage?

Seen, he does not come,
move, but seems forever there,
dimensionless, dumb,
in the windless noon's hot glare.

More scarred than others
these years since the trap maimed him,
pain slants his withers,
drawing up the crooked limb.

Then he is gone, whole,
without urgency, from sight,
as buzzards control,
imperceptibly, their flight.

Buteo Regalis

His frailty descrete, the rodent turns, looks.
What sense first warns? The winging is unheard,
Unseen but as distant motion made whole,
Singular, slow, unbroken in its glide.
It veers, and veering, tilts broad-surfaced wings.
Aligned, the span bends to begin the dive
And falls, alternately white and russet,
Angle and curve, gathering momentum.

Pit Viper

The cordate head meanders through himself:
Metamorphosis. Slowly the new thing,
Kindled to flares along his length, curves out.
From the evergreen shade where he has lain,
Through inland seas and catacombs he moves.
Blurred eyes that ever see have seen him waste,
Acquire, and undiminished: have seen death—
Or simile—come nigh and overcome.
Alone among his kind, old, almost wise,
Mere hunger cannot urge him from this drowse.

Comparatives

Sunlit sea,
the drift of fronds,
and banners
of bobbing boats—
the seaside
of any day—
except: this
cold, bright body
of the fish
upon the planks,
the coil and
crescent of flesh
extending
just into death.

Even so,
in the distant,
inland sea,
a shadow runs,
radiant,
rude in the rock:
fossil fish,
fissure of bone
forever.
It is perhaps
the same thing,

an agony
twice perceived.

It is most like
wind on waves—
mere commotion,
mute and mean,
perceptible—
that is all.

Earth and I Gave You Turquoise

Earth and I gave you turquoise
    when you walked singing
We lived laughing in my house
    and told old stories
You grew ill when the owl cried
We will meet on Black Mountain

I will bring corn for planting
    and we will make fire
Children will come to your breast
    You will heal my heart
I speak your name many times
The wild cane remembers you

My young brother's house is filled
    I go there to sing
We have not spoken of you
    but our songs are sad
When Moon Woman goes to you
I will follow her white way

Tonight they dance near Chinle
    by the seven elms
There your loom whispered beauty
    They will eat mutton
and drink coffee till morning
You and I will not be there

I saw a crow by Red Rock
        standing on one leg
It was the black of your hair
        The years are heavy
I will ride the swiftest horse
You will hear the drumming hooves

Simile

What did we say to each other
that now we are as the deer
who walk in single file
with heads high
with ears forward
with eyes watchful
with hooves always placed on firm ground
in whose limbs there is latent flight

Walk on the Moon

For Henry Raymont,
21 July 1969

Extend, there where you venture and come back,
The edge of Time. Be it your farthest track.
Time in that distance wanes. What is *to be*,
That present verb, there in Tranquillity?

Four Notions of Love and Marriage

*For Judith and Richardson Morse,
their wedding*

1.

Formerly I thought of you twice,
as it were.
Presently I think of you once
and for all.

2.

I wish you well:
that you are the runners of a wild vine,
that you are the roan and russet of dusk,
that you are a hawk and the hawk's shadow,
that you are grown old in love and delight,
I wish you well.

3.

Be still, lovers.
When the moon falls away westward,
there is your story in the stars.

4.

In my regalia,
in moccasins,

with gourd and eagle-feather fan,
in my regalia
imagine me;
imagine that I sing
and dance at your wedding.

Plainview: 1

There in the hollow of the hills I see,
Eleven magpies stand away from me.

Low light upon the rim; a wind informs
This distance with a gathering of storms

And drifts in silver crescents on the grass,
Configurations that appear, and pass.

There falls a final shadow on the glare,
A stillness on the dark, erratic air.

I do not hear the longer wind that lows
Among the magpies. Silences disclose,

Until no rhythms of unrest remain,
Eleven magpies standing in the plain.

They are illusion—wind and rain revolve—
And they recede in darkness, and dissolve.

Plainview: 2

I saw an old Indian
At Saddle Mountain
He drank and dreamed of drinking
And a blue-black horse

Remember my horse running
    Remember my horse
Remember my horse running
    Remember my horse

Remember my horse wheeling
    Remember my horse
Remember my horse wheeling
    Remember my horse

Remember my horse blowing
    Remember my horse
Remember my horse blowing
    Remember my horse

Remember my horse standing
    Remember my horse
Remember my horse standing
    Remember my horse

Remember my horse hurting
    Remember my horse

Remember my horse hurting
Remember my horse

Remember my horse falling
Remember my horse
Remember my horse falling
Remember my horse

Remember my horse dying
Remember my horse
Remember my horse dying
Remember my horse

A horse is one thing
An Indian another
An old horse is old
An old Indian is sad

I saw an old Indian
At Saddle Mountain
He drank and dreamed of drinking
And a blue-black horse

Remember my horse running
Remember my horse
Remember my horse wheeling
Remember my horse

Remember my horse blowing
Remember my horse
Remember my horse standing
Remember my horse
Remember my horse hurting
Remember my horse
Remember my horse falling
Remember my horse
Remember my horse dying
Remember my horse
Remember my blue-black horse
Remember my blue-black horse
Remember my horse
Remember my horse
Remember
Remember

Plainview: 3

The sun appearing: a pendant
of clear cutbeads, flashing;
a drift of pollen and glitter
lapping, and overlapping night;
a prairie fire.

Plainview: 4

Johnny cake and venison and sassafras tea,
Johnny cake and venison and sassafras tea.

Just there another house, Poor Buffalo's house.
The paint is gone from the wood, and the people are
gone from the house. Once upon a time I saw the people
there, in the windows and the yard. An old woman
lived there, one of whose girlhood I have often dreamed.
She was Milly Durgan of Texas, and a Kiowa captive.

Aye, Milly Durgan, you've gone now to be
Away in the country and captivity;
Aye, Milly Durgan, you've gone from your home
Away to the prairie forever to roam.

The warm wind lies about the house in March,
and there is a music in it, as I have heard, an
American song.

And it's ladies to the center
and it's gents around the row,
And we'll rally round the canebrake
and shoot the buffalo.

The lines in italics are from two American folk songs, "The Texian
Boys," and "Shoot the Buffalo."

The Fear of Bo-talee

Bo-talee rode easily among his enemies, once, twice,
three—and four times. And all who saw him were
amazed, for he was utterly without fear; so it seemed.
But afterwards he said: Certainly I was afraid. I was
afraid of the fear in the eyes of my enemies.

The Story of a Well-Made Shield

Now in the dawn before it dies, the eagle swings
low and wide in a great arc, curving downward
to the place of origin. There is no wind, but there
is a long roaring on the air. It is like the wind—
nor is it quite like the wind—but more powerful.

The Horse that Died of Shame

*Once there was a man who owned a fine hunting
horse. It was black and fast and afraid of nothing.
When it was turned upon an enemy it charged in a
straight line and struck at full speed; the man
need have no hand upon the rein. But, you know,
that man knew fear. Once during a charge he turned
that animal from its course. That was a bad thing.
The hunting horse died of shame.*

From *The Way to Rainy Mountain*

In the one color of the horse there were many
colors. And that evening it wheeled, riderless, and broke
away into the long distance, running at full speed. And
so it does again and again in my dreaming. It seems to
concentrate all color and light into the final moment of
its life, until it streaks the vision plane and is indefinite,
and shines vaguely like the gathering of March light
to a storm.

The Delight Song of Tsoai-talee

I am a feather on the bright sky
I am the blue horse that runs in the plain
I am the fish that rolls, shining, in the water
I am the shadow that follows a child
I am the evening light, the lustre of meadows
I am an eagle playing with the wind
I am a cluster of bright beads
I am the farthest star
I am the cold of the dawn
I am the roaring of the rain
I am the glitter on the crust of the snow
I am the long track of the moon in a lake
I am a flame of four colors
I am a deer standing away in the dusk
I am a field of sumac and the pomme blanche
I am an angle of geese in the winter sky
I am the hunger of a young wolf
I am the whole dream of these things

You see, I am alive, I am alive
I stand in good relation to the earth
I stand in good relation to the gods
I stand in good relation to all that is beautiful
I stand in good relation to the daughter of Tsen-tainte
You see, I am alive, I am alive

Before an Old Painting of the Crucifixion

The Mission Carmel,
June 1960

I ponder how He died, despairing once.
I've heard the cry subside in vacant skies,
In clearings where no other was. Despair,
Which, in the vibrant wake of utterance,
Resides in desolate calm, preoccupies,
Though it is still. There is no solace there.

That calm inhabits wilderness, the sea,
And where no peace inheres but solitude;
Near death it most impends. It was for Him,
Absurd and public in His agony,
Inscrutably itself, nor misconstrued,
Nor metaphrased in art or pseudonym:

A vague contagion. Old, the mural fades . . .
Reminded of the fainter sea I scanned,
I recollect: How mute in constancy!
I could not leave the wall of palisades
Till cormorants returned my eyes on land.
The mural but implies eternity:

Not death, but silence after death is change.
Judean hills, the endless afternoon,
The farther groves and arbors seasonless
But fix the mind within the moment's range.

Where evening would obscure our sorrow soon,
There shines too much a sterile loveliness.

No imprecisions of commingled shade,
No shimmering deceptions of the sun,
Herein no semblances remark the cold
Unhindered swell of time, for time is stayed.
The Passion wanes into oblivion,
And time and timelessness confuse, I'm told.

These centuries removed from either fact
Have lain upon the critical expanse
And been of little consequence. The void
Is calendared in stone; the human act,
Outrageous, is in vain. The hours advance
Like flecks of foam borne landward and destroyed.

Headwaters

Noon in the intermountain plain:
There is scant telling of the marsh—
A log, hollow and weather-stained,
An insect at the mouth, and moss—
Yet waters rise against the roots,
Stand brimming to the stalks. What moves?
What moves on this archaic force
Was wild and welling at the source.

Rainy Mountain Cemetery

Most is your name the name of this dark stone.
Deranged in death, the mind to be inheres
Forever in the nominal unknown,
The wake of nothing audible he hears
Who listens here and now to hear your name.

The early sun, red as a hunter's moon,
Runs in the plain. The mountain burns and shines;
And silence is the long approach of noon
Upon the shadow that your name defines—
And death this cold, black density of stone.

Angle of Geese

How shall we adorn
Recognition with our speech?—
Now the dead firstborn
Will lag in the wake of words.

Custom intervenes;
We are civil, something more:
More than language means,
The mute presence mulls and marks.

Almost of a mind,
We take measure of the loss;
I am slow to find
The mere margin of repose.

And one November
It was longer in the watch,
As if forever,
Of the huge ancestral goose.

So much symmetry!—
Like the pale angle of time
And eternity.
The great shape labored and fell.

Quit of hope and hurt,
It held a motionless gaze
Wide of time, alert,
On the dark distant flurry.

II

The Gourd Dancer

For Jill

The Gourd Dancer

Mammedaty, 1880–1932

1. The Omen

Another season centers on this place.
Like memory the blood congeals in it;
Like memory the sun recedes in time
Into the hazy, southern distances.

A vagrant heat hangs on the dark river,
And shadows turn like smoke. An owl ascends
Among the branches, clattering, remote
Within its motion, intricate with age.

2. The Dream

Mammedaty saw to the building of this house.
Just there, by the arbor, he made a camp in the old way.
And in the evening when the hammers had fallen silent
and there were frogs and crickets in the black grass—
and a low, hectic wind upon the pale, slanting plane
of the moon's light—he settled deep down in his mind
to dream. He dreamed of dreaming, and of the summer
breaking upon his spirit, as drums break upon the
intervals of the dance, and of the gleaming gourds.

3. The Dance

Dancing,
He dreams, he dreams—

The long wind glances, moves
Forever as a music to the mind;
The gourds are flashes of the sun.
He takes the inward, mincing steps
That conjure old processions and returns.

Dancing,
His moccasins,
His sash and bandolier
Contain him in insignia;
His fan is powerful, concise
According to his agile hand,
And holds upon the deep, ancestral air.

4. The Giveaway

Someone spoke his name, Mammedaty, in which
his essence was and is. It was a serious matter that his
name should be spoken there in the circle, among the
many people, and he was thoughtful, full of wonder,
and aware of himself and of his name. He walked
slowly to the summons, looking into the eyes of the man
who summoned him. For a moment they held each
other in close regard, and all about them there was
excitement and suspense.

Then a boy came suddenly into the circle, leading
a black horse. The boy ran, and the horse after him.
He brought the horse up short in front of Mammedaty,
and the horse wheeled and threw its head and cut
its eyes in the wild way. And it blew hard and quivered
in its hide so that light ran, rippling, upon its shoulders
and its flanks—and then it stood still and was calm.
Its mane and tail were fixed in braids and feathers, and
a bright red chief's blanket was draped in a roll over
its withers. The boy placed the reins in Mammedaty's
hands. And all of this was for Mammedaty, in his honor,
as even now it is in the telling, and will be, as long as
there are those who imagine him in his name.

New World

First Man,
behold:
the earth
glitters
with leaves;
the sky
glistens
with rain.
Pollen
is borne
on winds
that low
and lean
upon
mountains.
Cedars
blacken
the slopes—
and pines.

2.

At dawn
eagles
hie and

hover
above
the plain
where light
gathers
in pools.
Grasses
shimmer
and shine.
Shadows
withdraw
and lie
away
like smoke.

3.

At noon
turtles
enter
slowly
into
the warm
dark loam.
Bees hold
the swarm.
Meadows

recede
through planes
of heat
and pure
distance.

4.

At dusk
the gray
foxes
stiffen
in cold;
blackbirds
are fixed
in the
branches.
Rivers
follow
the moon,
the long
white track
of the
full moon.

The Stalker

Sampt'e drew the string back and back until he felt
the bow wobble in his hand, and he let the arrow go.
It shot across the long light of the morning and struck
the black face of a stone in the meadow; it glanced
then away towards the west, limping along in the air;
and then it settled down in the grass and lay still.
Sampt'e approached; he looked at it with wonder and was
wary; honestly he believed that the arrow might take flight
again; so much of his life did he give into it.

Carriers of the Dream Wheel

This is the Wheel of Dreams
Which is carried on their voices,
By means of which their voices turn
And center upon being.
It encircles the First World,
This powerful wheel.
They shape their songs upon the wheel
And spin the names of the earth and sky,
The aboriginal names.
They are old men, or men
Who are old in their voices,
And they carry the wheel among the camps,
Saying: Come, come,
Let us tell the old stories,
Let us sing the sacred songs.

The Eagle-Feather Fan

The eagle is my power,
And my fan is an eagle.
It is strong and beautiful
In my hand. And it is real.
My fingers hold upon it
As if the beaded handle
Were the twist of bristlecone.
The bones of my hand are fine
And hollow; the fan bears them.
My hand veers in the thin air
Of the summits. All morning
It scuds on the cold currents;
All afternoon it circles
To the singing, to the drums.

The Colors of Night

1. *White*

An old man's son was killed far away in the Staked
Plains. When the old man heard of it he went there
and gathered up the bones. Thereafter, wherever the
old man ventured, he led a dark hunting horse which
bore the bones of his son on its back. And the old man
said to whomever he saw: "You see how it is that now
my son consists in his bones, that his bones are polished
and so gleam like glass in the light of the sun and moon,
that he is very beautiful."

2. *Yellow*

There was a boy who drowned in the river, near the
grove of thirty-two bois d'arc trees. The light of the
moon lay like a path on the water, and a glitter of
low brilliance shone in it. The boy looked at it and was
enchanted. He began to sing a song that he had never
heard before; only then, once, did he hear it in his heart,
and it was borne like a cloud of down upon his voice.
His voice entered into the bright track of the moon,
and he followed after it. For a time he made his way
along the path of the moon, singing. He paddled with
his arms and legs and felt his body rocking down into
the swirling water. His vision ran along the path of light
and reached across the wide night and took hold of the
moon. And across the river, where the path led into the
shadows of the bank, a black dog emerged from the river,

shivering and shaking the water from its hair. All night
it stood in the waves of grass and howled the
full moon down.

3. Brown

On the night before a flood, the terrapins move to high
ground. How is it that they know? Once there was a boy
who took up a terrapin in his hands and looked at it
for a long time, as hard as he could look. He succeeded
in memorizing the terrapin's face, but he failed to see
how it was that the terrapin knew anything at all.

4. Red

There was a man who had got possession of a powerful
medicine. And by means of this medicine he made a
woman out of sumac leaves and lived with her for a time.
Her eyes flashed, and her skin shone like pipestone.
But the man abused her, and so his medicine failed.
The woman was caught up in a whirlwind and blown
apart. Then nothing was left of her but a thousand
withered leaves scattered in the plain.

5. Green

A young girl awoke one night and looked out into the
moonlit meadow. There appeared to be a tree; but it was

only an appearance; there was a shape made of smoke; but it was only an appearance; there was a tree.

6. *Blue*

One night there appeared a child in the camp. No one had ever seen it before. It was not bad-looking, and it spoke a language that was pleasant to hear, though none could understand it. The wonderful thing was that the child was perfectly unafraid, as if it were at home among its own people. The child got on well enough, but the next morning it was gone, as suddenly as it had appeared. Everyone was troubled. But then it came to be understood that the child never was, and everyone felt better. "After all," said an old man, "how can we believe in the child? It gave us not one word of sense to hold on to. What we saw, if indeed we saw anything at all, must have been a dog from a neighboring camp, or a bear that wandered down from the high country."

7. *Purple*

There was a man who killed a buffalo bull to no purpose, only he wanted its blood on his hands. It was a great, old, noble beast, and it was a long time blowing its life away. On the edge of the night the people gathered themselves up in their grief and shame. Away in the west they could see the hump and spine of the huge beast which lay dying along the edge of the world. They could see its bright blood run into the sky, where it dried, darkening, and was at last flecked with flakes of light.

8. Black

There was a woman whose hair was long and heavy and black and beautiful. She drew it about her like a shawl and so divided herself from the world that not even Age could find her. Now and then she steals into the men's societies and fits her voice into their holiest songs. And always, just there, is a shadow which the firelight cannot cleave.

The Monoliths

The wind lay upon me.
The monoliths were there
in the long light, standing
cleanly apart from time.

North Dakota, North Light

The cold comes about
among the sheer, lucent planes.

Rabbits rest in the foreground;
the sky is clenched upon them.

A glassy wind glances
from the ball of bone in my wrist
even as I brace myself,
and I cannot conceive
of summer;

and another man in me
stands for it,
wills even to remain,

figurative, fixed,

among the hard, hunchbacked rabbits,
among the sheer, shining planes.

Winter Holding off the Coast
of North America

This dread is like a calm,
And colorless. Nothing
Lies in the stricken palm
But the dead cold coming.

Out there, beyond the floes,
On the thin, pewter plane,
The polar currents close,
And stiffen, and remain.

To a Child Running
with Outstretched Arms
in Canyon de Chelly

You are small and intense
In your excitement, whole,
Embodied in delight.
The backdrop is immense;

The sand banks break and roll
Through cleavages of light
And shadow. You embrace
The spirit of this place.

49

Long Shadows at Dulce

1.

September is a long
Illusion of itself;
The elders bide their time.

2.

The sheep camps are lively
With children. The slim girls,
The limber girls, recline.

3.

November is the flesh
And blood of the black bear,
Dusk its bone and marrow.

4.

In the huddled horses
That know of perfect cold
There is calm, like sorrow.

III

Anywhere Is a Street into the Night

For Brit

Crows in a Winter Composition

This morning the snow,
The soft distances
Beyond the trees
In which nothing appeared—
Nothing appeared—
The several silences,
Imposed one upon another,
Were unintelligible.

I was therefore ill at ease
When the crows came down,
Whirling down and calling,
Into the yard below
And stood in a mindless manner
On the gray, luminous crust,
Altogether definite, composed,
In the bright enmity of my regard,
In the hard nature of crows.

Anywhere Is a Street into the Night

Desire will come of waiting
Here at this window—I bring
An old urgency to bear
Upon me, and anywhere
Is a street into the night,
Deliverance and delight—
And evenly it will pass
Like this image on the glass.

For the Old Man for Drawing,
Dead at Eighty-Nine

". . . at ninety I shall have penetrated
to the essence of all things . . ."
HOKUSAI

This late drawing:
in these deft lines
a corpulent merchant reclines
against a pillow.
Here is a fragile equation
for which there is an Asian origin.
In this and that and another stroke
there is something like possibility
succeeding to infinity.
In another year there might have been here
not apparently
a corpulent merchant and his pillow
but really
three long winds converging on the dawn.

Abstract: Old Woman in a Room

For Olga Sergeevna Akhmanova

Here is no place of easy consequence
But where you come to reckon recompense;

And here the vacancy in which are met
The vague contingencies of your regret.

Here is the will's disease. And otherwise
Here is no reparation in surmise.

Here the white light that touches your white hair
Replaces you in darkness and despair.

And here where age constricts you, death is dear,
And essences of anguish stay you here.

That Woman and This Woman

That woman: she is composed—
has indeed composed herself—
among the shapes and shadows
that call for her,
for which she is the complement.
She brings, with her bag of tricks,
everything into place.
She sits at a small, round table,
rather far away, against the sunlit wall.
I see that her mouth is expressive,
that she is certainly beautiful.
She does not suspect
the existence of so many things
that are unlike my regard
in one way or another.
Such things, if indeed they existed for her,
she should put aside at once and forever.
She is certainly beautiful,
and one cannot help himself—
he must desire her.
But he must also understand
that she consists in his desire.

This woman: she laughs easily,
and so does she love.
Just now she is of a mind
to raise the hem of her dress to her eyes
and place her thighs to the wind.

The Burning

In the numb, numberless days
There were disasters in the distance,
Strange upheavals. No one understood them.
At night the sky was scored with light,
For the far planes of the planet buckled and burned.
In the dawns were intervals of darkness
On the scorched sky, clusters of clouds and eclipse,
And cinders descending.
Nearer in the noons
The air lay low and ominous and inert.
And eventually at evening, or morning, or midday,
At the sheer wall of the wood,
Were shapes in the shadows approaching,
Always, and always alien and alike.
And in the foreground the fields were fixed in fire,
And the flames flowered in our flesh.

The Wound

The wound gaped open;
It was remarkably like the wedge of an orange
when it is split, spurting.
He wanted to close the wound with a kiss,
to graft his mouth to the warm, wet tissue.
He kept about the wound, waiting
and deeply disturbed,
his fascination
like the inside of the wound itself,
deep, as deep almost as the life principle,
the irresistible force of being.
The force lay there in the rupture of the flesh,
there in the center of the wound.

Had he been God,
he should Himself have inflicted the wound;
and he should have taken the wound gently,
gently in his hands, and placed it
among the most brilliant wildflowers
in the meadows of the mountains.

Forms of the Earth at Abiquiu

For Georgia O'Keeffe

I imagine the time of our meeting
There among the forms of the earth at Abiquiu,
And other times that followed from the one—
An easy conjugation of stories,
And late luncheons of wine and cheese.
All around there were beautiful objects,
Clean and precise in their beauty, like bone.
Indeed, bone: a snake in the filaments of bone,
The skulls of cows and sheep;
And the many smooth stones in the window,
In the flat winter light, were beautiful.
I wanted to feel the sun in the stones—
The ashen, far-flung winter sun—
But this I did not tell you, I believe,
But I believe that after all you knew.
And then, in those days, too,
I made you the gift of a small, brown stone,
And you described it with the tips of your fingers
And knew at once that it was beautiful—
At once, accordingly you knew,
As you knew the forms of the earth at Abiquiu:
That time involves them and they bear away,
Beautiful, various, remote,
In failing light, and the coming of cold.